D0036148

ROBERT M. DRAKE

EMPTY BOTTLES FULL *of* STORIES

r.h. Sin

*Cover illustration
by Hannah Olson*

Andrews McMeel
PUBLISHING®

also by r.h. Sin

Whiskey Words & a Shovel

Whiskey Words & a Shovel II

Whiskey Words & a Shovel III

Rest in the Mourning

A Beautiful Composition of Broken

Algedonic

She Felt Like Feeling Nothing

Planting Gardens in Graves

Planting Gardens in Graves Volume Two

Planting Gardens in Graves Volume Three

We Hope This Reaches You in Time
with Samantha King Holmes

ALSO BY ROBERT M. DRAKE
The King Is Dead
Dawn of Mayhem
Seeds of Wrath
Moon Matrix
The Great Artist
Dead Pop Art
Beautiful Chaos 2
Chaos Theory
Star Theory
Light Theory
Moon Theory
Gravity: A Novel
Seeds of Chaos
Beautiful and Damned
Beautiful Chaos
A Brilliant Madness
Black Butterfly
Broken Flowers
Spaceship
Science

THE CURSE

THE CURSE CONTENTS

TWO PEOPLE

Distance has a funny way
of reminding you
how close two people
could either grow apart
or grow closer together.

And now you're gone
and I am here

wondering

if letting you go
was the right thing
to do.

I just hope
that somewhere,
in some thread of time,

you're doing okay.

So, in the meantime,
I will be thinking
of you
and I will be missing you

and I will be hoping
that some way,

some how,
you'd find
the inspiration needed
to find your way

back home.

WHAT PEOPLE NEED

People want to heal.

They want to know
how the stars
ended up on their hands,

how the comets soar
through their eyes,

and how the flowers grow
within their hearts . . .

when all hope is lost.

They want other people,
like you,

to feel the force of things,
to understand the magnitude
of the falling heart,

of the breaking heart.

They want to know
they're not alone . . .

that their hands
were meant to fill
other hands

and that the black holes
in their souls
lead to the most
beautiful of places.

Like the ones
you can't outrun.

Like the ones
you gravitate toward.

My child,
this is what they want.

This is what brings
people closer.

Know,
how some people have lost
their way,
but please believe,
that ultimately,

we all obtain the goodness
of the gods.

We all want to be saved
and
we are all looking for
reasons to love.

My child,
before I leave you,

KNOW,

that the world is hard,
that people are soft,
and all of us
are terribly looking for ways
NOT to shatter.

HARD EDGES

Beneath my hard edges.

Beneath my torn,
battered heart.

Beneath my sunbathed flesh
and these worn bones.

Please believe,
that somewhere in me,

there is a love song
and it is the kind
you listen to

while driving
back home.

WHAT WE DO

It's what we do.

The same things
over and over.

Where risk blooms
and the pain of growth

stings

from the marrow
of the bone.

From the moment of birth
till death . . .

it is all,
after all,

about the meaning.

The in-between,
the moments of chaos,
the ones where it feels
as if our lives
are falling apart.

That brink of losing it,
all of it.

Where there is pain,
there is love.

Where there is failure,
there is success.

Where there is war,
there is peace.

It is what we do
from start to finish . . .

not where time pivots
the two.

It is what you collect,
not what you let go.

It is what you feel,
not what you think
you feel.

Real is real
and what you do
means nothing

if you do not understand
why you do
the things you have
done,

and what you
have given up
and lost

for a chance to love.

WHOM YOU LOVE

It's about
the way you
love,
not whom you
love.

Whom you spend
your life with,
not whom you know.

The same way
it's about
the things you do,

not what you say.

Know the difference.

That's what makes you
who you are.

MY COUNTRY

O country, my country.

I see your people
feeling the wrath
of the wealthy.

The wrath
of those who don't see
the future as a promise
but as their doom.

O country, my country.

I see your people
without the grasp of hope,
drowning in the bitter bowl,
the one that the great beast,
the great American corporation,
feasts on.

O country, my country.

I see your banks,
your health care,
your dream being sold
to the poor,

to the men and the women
who are robbed
of their own place
in the system
they helped build.

O country, my country.

I see the land severely wounded.
I see its blood flooding,
the cities,
the agriculture,
and the oceans.

I see the tears of those
who feel . . .
filling the graves of their ancestors,
the ones who know
the truth behind this promise
of justice,
of equality, and of the pursuit
of happiness.

O country, my country.

More wars, more death,
and more suffering.

The three comrades
are stretching toward other countries . . .
convincing them to follow,
that this truth
is holy.

O country, my country.

Does life end
the moment we step outside?
Does life begin
the moment we are invited
to stand with them?

So the people you collect
look up
and the 1 percent
continue to look down?

O country, my country.
I see the people being told
how to think,
what to think,
when to think,
and where.

I see the people enslaved
by your Internet,
your televisions,
your mobile phones,
and your radios.

O country, my country.

I plead for freedom,
that of speech,
religion, and culture.

I seek the truth
we've never been told.

The truth of your past
and how the natives were killed
to transform you
for their democracy.

O country, my country.

I see no peace.
I see you in pain.
I see the sadness in your eyes
and you see it in ours.

I see no responsibility,
no courage, no guts,
no true love.

O country, my country.

The propaganda is endless.

The hate is too great
and too dangerous
and the love is too dim
and out of reach.

The game is too hard
and we have been cheated
from the first breath
of life.

O country, my country.
Please let me go.
Please set me free.
Please do not kill the youth.

Do not kill the inspiration,
the rebellion of children,
the dream,
and the feeling the people need
to go on.

Please understand
that without us
there is no you.

Please understand
that we, too, bleed
and have bled
for our families.

Please understand
that like you,

we, too,

have much to offer the world.

O country, my country.

Please love your people.

*That is
the only way
we both*

will survive.

MUCH SENSE

I get you,

you don't know
how you feel.

Well,

I will tell you this:

the world doesn't
make much sense

without

the people
you love.

BLOOMING

No matter what they say,

know,

that all good things
take time to bloom

and all sadness
is not a waste
of life.

Sadness,
like happiness,

is delicate and temporary.

So here's to you
for being true . . .

for being beautiful.

The sun is the brightest thing
in the sky
and so are you.

Be easy on yourself.
Be cool.

A flower is still
a flower . . .

no matter
what it goes through

and no matter

where it decides

to bloom.

TOO LATE

You've gone through
so many lovers

that you begin to forget
what it is you love
about being in love.

It becomes useless,
this idea of it,
of finding it,
of keeping it,
and believing it was meant
to save you.

*(As we all tend to believe
from time to time.)*

Then, one night,
out of the silent flares
from the moon . . .

you discover her.

A woman filled
with cleverness and adventure.

A woman filled with passion,
charm, and an appetite
for life.

You take her
or rather, she takes you
into her past,
into your past,

to begin from within.

And this time,
as you do,
as you're reborn from the ashes
of your old life.

You remember her
and thank her,

this rare woman, who nearly
saved you.

You thank her
for showing you the way.

You thank her
for pulling your feet
out of the grave.

And the funny thing is,
how soon enough,
you'll ignore her.

You'll add her to the banks
of your memory
with the rest of them.

You'll go on,
and experience

other

average lovers once again.

And it always happens
like this:

you'll remember her
when it's too late,
and you'll lose your mind,
and your heart
just as swiftly
as she returned it.

You'll beat yourself up
for the rest of your life
for losing
your one true love.

Damn.

Too often
this is how it ends . . .

and too often
do we, as people,

only *appreciate* someone

once

they are gone.

WHAT THEY DON'T TEACH
IN SCIENCE CLASS

Because missing you
is a science

and I'm still

a scientist

and the chemistry between

the heart and love

will always
be a lie.

THE ISSUE

The issue is,

you think
you own love forever.

You think
the people around you
will have it, too.

Don't waste any time.

Tell them
you need them,

show them
why now is important.

Why now is special.

We might never get
this chance

ever again.
The past is always growing
and time
is just another metaphor

that represents
all the people

we've lost.

RUN WITH YOU

I don't know
how many times
you've been
broken

and I don't know
how many times
you've fallen

but I do know one thing.

You make me
want to run with you.

You make me
want to find
that one place,

where I can surrender
and make sense
of all this love

I have contained
within.

I want to run away
with you . . .

somewhere far . . .

where the wolves
have gone missing

and the butterflies
continuously spread their wings.

I want to find this place
with you . . .

and I want to grow
old there.

That's all.

I THINK, I DON'T THINK

I think
you like the idea
of feeling
too much,
of experiencing
too much

and letting the things
inside you
float away.

I think
you want people
to notice you

but want others
to think that
isolation pumps through
your veins.

I think
you care
too much
but you pretend
as if
nothing bothers you.

I think
you want people
to miss you
but only
the right ones.

I think
you like breaking
apart

but only because
you know by morning

you'll be
yourself again.

I think
you like being chased
because you want
to be saved
and loved

with the same intensity
an earthquake
would bring.

I think
you want the world
to remember you
but you don't have
the slightest clue
on becoming memorable.

I think
you want delicate hands
to surf over
your skin

but you think
you're too hard
for soft hands.

I think
of all these things
and it couldn't be
more true,
that like me,
you just need someone
to catch you
and tell you
how much they know you—
to reveal
little things about you,

that you
yourself ignore.

I think
the star in you
wants to give light
to other people

and I think

I need it
to help me
find my way.

And, like you,
I think
and feel these things
deeply . . .

and I know we need
each other . . .

if ever,
we think
we want

a proper shot

at love.

STORIES

I know
there are
two sides
to the world—
two stories.

One good
and one bad,

and
you shouldn't ignore
the bad.

You should know it
but don't fall into it.

The world is beautiful,
life is beautiful,
and hatred shouldn't be
carried.

So please go on
gently
and always remember
to let all things
that weigh you down

go.

TOO MUCH OF ANYTHING IS BAD

Too much war.
Too much slavery.
Too much famine.
Too much death.
Too much suffering.
Too much pain.
Too much nothingness.

All around,
filling the room.

Too much laughter.
Too much peace.
Too much comfort.
Too much togetherness.
Too much love.
Too much life.
Too much passion.

People, moments, and life
will show you
how too much
of anything can be dangerous.

They will make you

either

feel more or less.

The beautiful gift
and curse of being human,
to give and to take away.

To build or destroy.

The same way people,
both men and women,
dead or alive,

have gone through
and/or will go through

too much of too much.

Too much emptiness.
Too much confusion.
Too much to hold.
Too much to let go.

You won't be
the same person
after you've seen
what you're meant
to see . . .

and how could you?

The world is both
light and dark
and only those
with their eyes open
see

and find their way.

It is both

a curse and a blessing
to feel things

so deeply

and too much of anything

will always be
too much

for you to bear.

Always.

SORROW RISES

The heart
is sometimes
a liar,

for at times,

it promises happiness
but too often,

it leaves you
alone

with nothing more
than sorrow.

What a terrible monster
to feed.

It wants and wants and wants
and almost always,

does it leave you
empty-handed
with nothing left
to hold.

A GIRL I ONCE KNEW

She had tragic eyes—
sad eyes
as if she had seen
too much
or had too many stars

die

within the edge
of her pupils.

Large, faraway eyes,
as if
all the things
she had lived through
meant nothing
without the people
she loved.

Without a word
she speaks
and tells me
all the things
I need to hear,

the things
I need
to ease the pain
a little.

With a few blinks
she calms my storms,
the mad wolves
rioting inside of my brain,

the ones who feed off
my heart,
courage,
and inspiration.

Her eyes wander,
they take the whole
goddamn feeling,
the whole
goddamn moment . . .

as if
she drank the ocean
within my beating chest,
and now
I'm lost at sea.

My life is nothing,
this is what I tell
my comrades.

That without her
I'm just another fool
searching for the pieces
that may
or may not

complete me.

Those eyes,
beautiful and lost.

Those eyes,
piercing and soft.

Those eyes,
sane and mad.

Like the gentle doubt
I carry
throughout my life.

I'm a fool,
I say,

and like the fool
that I am,

I follow
and I walk
toward her darkness—
where all the dying stars
end up.

Where the light
can't escape
and where all
the lost people go
to be found.

Those eyes,
beautiful and lost.

Those eyes,
piercing and soft.

Those eyes,
sane and mad.

And with one look

I am lost . . .

forever.

LETTER TO MY DAUGHTER

Listen to the way
life slowly walks
out of her body.

If there is any kind
of music
to be appreciated,

then it is there,
between the beats
of her heart

and the quiet exhale
of her breath.

So please,
love her
and love her well.

She is not meant
to live forever

but the idea
is to make her feel
as if
she is the center
of the universe . . .

every single day.

Amen.

ALWAYS IN ME

Always in me,
there is a moon
and some nights
it lights my sky,

while other nights
it emphasizes
my brokenness.

Always in me,
there is a star
and some nights
it caves within itself,

while other nights
it expands
to devour other worlds.

Always in me,
there is an ocean
and sometimes

it's calm,
while other nights
it drowns the people
I love.

Always in me,
there is a garden
of flowers
and some nights
it blooms,

while other nights
it grants me strength
over my weaknesses.

Always in me,
there is a thunderstorm
and some nights
it understands me,

while other nights
it takes my breath away.

Always in me,
there is a great sadness
and some nights

it hurts,
while other nights
it is silenced
by laughter.

Always in me,
there are sides of you
and some nights
you don't have me,

while other nights
I can't escape
what you've done.

Always in me,
there are maps
and some nights
I wander away,

while other nights
they lead me straight
to you.

Always in me,
stay with me,
for some nights
are better than others

and other nights
stay the same as before.

Always in me,
stay with me,

for some nights
people see you
for who you are,
while other nights
they see themselves
in the things
they want to see.

Always in me,
stay with me,
and never leave my side,

for some nights
I am yours,
while other nights
you are mine.

Stay with me.
Always in me.
Always with me.

Always
by my side.

TOO MUCH DARKNESS

Sometimes,
I feel
like I have too much
to offer.

Too much light
and too much darkness.

Too much repetitiveness
and too much contradiction.

Too much love
and too little
time to explore it.

Too much heart
and too much inspiration
to change that look
in your eyes.

Too much flame
and too much passion
to control.

I feel the people.
I feel the pain.
I feel the breath
of the ocean in me.

ROBERT M. DRAKE   56

And because of it
I carry too much
of *too much*
for my own good.

I am still,
and the weight of it all
is beautiful.

And sometimes,
among all things,

I feel like
a dying star.

Like I am
collapsing within myself,
devouring every planet,
every person,
and every moment

I . . .

have ever known.

TWO SIDES

There are two sides
of me . . .

for example,
one side of me knows
what to do,
while the other side
of me doesn't.

So there are days
when I do
want to stay

but then

there are days
when I want to go
as far as possible.

And I don't know
which side of me
works best with you,

in fact,
I don't know at all

but

I do know one thing.

Both sides of me think of you
all the time

and they miss you
whenever

you're not around.

OBEY OBEY OBEY

Obey what you feel
and know
that your heart will
always lead you
in the right direction.

Put your trust
in the atoms
inside of you.

Believe in them,
know them . . .

they are connected
for a reason

after all.

FAME IS DEAD

Fame.

What is fame?
The knowing?
The recognition?
Is fame power?
True power?

Why do people fight for it?

Why do people
crave being accepted,
appreciated,
and loved by many?

I never understood this
and to be honest,

I'm not sure
how anyone could even
want this type of commitment.

Fame.
Please no thank you.

I like myself.
I like where I am.
I like the fact
that I am unknown
although,
my work has been shared
by millions.

Choice.

It is my choice.
However I want to proceed
or not
is *ultimately my decision.*

It's up to me,
up to you.

I want to stay in the shadows.
I want to stay
where all things that go

ignored remain
where they do go die . . .
but be in the light
just enough
to be remembered.

Not in present
but in the past.

I want people to say,

"Hey I remember him.
His books were great;
they inspired me."

That's all I really want.

I want the eight-year-old kid
to pick up my book
and start writing,
because of me.

To me,
that is more important
than fame.

It is legendary
to inspire someone
to be more.

To believe in themselves . . .
the same way I have
in myself.

I want to be a champion
of the underdog.

Of the nine-to-fivers.

The ones who are trying
to break through
and make something out
of themselves.

I want to be a champion
to the ones
who believe people
can change
once they believe to accept
how easy it is to do so.

I want to represent
the ones
who are near the finish line
but for some reason
they finish second
instead of first.

They are still winners
for not giving up.

So fame,
is it needed to succeed?

Is being popular the answer?

No, it's not.

It's a distraction.
It's an illusion
and it pulls you away
from what really matters.

So to say
that I want to be famous
is completely irrelevant.

For one,
I don't like being filmed.
I don't like being photographed.

I tried it
and didn't like it.

So why should I do
something I don't want to?

That's not love.
That's not self-righteous.

To sell yourself
to sell more books?

I still remind myself
to find myself,
although millions of people
follow what it is
I stand for.

The truth is,

I still don't know who I am
but hey,
I'm working on it, right?
And it's a struggle
I go through every day.
The same as everyone else,
and that doesn't mean anything,
other than the fact
that *I'm just like you.*

I'm the same person
I have always been
and I always will be.

A million followers or not.

I'm still the same
young boy looking for a way out.
Looking for a way in . . .

that is,
into my own head
and my own heart
and being known has nothing
to do with it.

I'm still searching
for all the things
that bring me happiness.

It is the pursuit
that drives me
all along.

SOCIETY

We blame society
but we are society.

Teach the children
to be better,
to be different.

The world
is full of
second chances.

We could still
save our home

and we could still
change our hearts

to create
a better tomorrow.

REJOICE IS PERFECT

Genocide is not profitable.
Destruction is not beautiful.

Death may bring peace
but not under the cloth of violence.

Please save our people.

Please heal our children,
women, and men.

Please bring hope
back into our lives.

We seek peace, not war.
We seek love, not hatred.
We seek togetherness,
not isolation.

We need one another.
We need trust, change,
and revolution.

We need humanity
to crawl itself back
to our hearts.
(Where it originally came from.)

We need hands
rich of life
and not death
and emptiness.

We need rejoice.

Rejoice.
Rejoice.

Pain is not the celebrity.

Let us,
the people who feel
not worship the wrath,
the control of the banks.

Let us,
the people who love
brace together
and overcome their hate.

Give us back our people.
Give us back the love
we once had for ourselves.

Give us back our dreams
you stole.

Give us back our confidence.

Give us back everything
that belongs to us . . .

and give it back with interest.

There's still
so much we can do
with whatever bit

they give
us back.

STORMS

Summer rainstorms,
calm seashores,

and gentle nights
full of stars.

And I think,

this is where
the year ends

but this must be
how the chaos of me

begins.

B. OBAMA

I did a post once
about Obama.

After that
I could tell
how many of you
loved him
and how many of you
hated him.

I don't know why
each side is on
each side.

I wrote about him
because I was inspired
at the very least
by his farewell speech.

He said,

"Yes, we can.
Yes, we did.
Yes, we can."

The crowd raged,
they raged in light
and love, they raged.

Now back to my post.

I found this pic of him
throwing a football
in the oval office.

I had never seen a president
do something *so humanizing.*

It inspired me a little more.

I wrote "legacy"
on the caption, across the feeds . . .
for millions to see.

Out of good things
sometimes
come bad things.

With a heart full of positivity
sometimes hatred
isn't too far away.

Many of my readers were angry.

Upset because I made a post
out of respect to our president,
to our leader,

regardless of what he has done,
whether good or bad.

Many began to unfollow me,
which I came to this conclusion
after that.

If you want this world to heal,
then we must all be open
to the opinions of others.

We must all respect
one another as equals.

How in the world
do you expect to function,
to earn peoples' hearts?

Put it like this,
now if you have a friend
who appreciates something
you don't,

you're going to unfriend them
over it?

Perhaps not, right?
But it's the same idea.

I honored Obama
and got hate for it?

Well, my old friends,
that says more about you
than it does . . . about me.

Overcome the hatred.
Overcome the narrow path.

Not everyone is going
to agree with you.

Not everyone is going
to feel the same way.

GET OVER YOURSELF . . .

and let in
instead of out.

Yes, you can.
Yes, you did.
Yes, you can.

THE REALIZATION

How could you
think you are weak

when every time you break,

you come back stronger
than before?

PIERCING SOUL

I can see it
in your eyes,

you're hiding something
or maybe even
someone.

So keep telling yourself
you don't need me
to help you

because

one day,
I'm going to find you
and you won't lose
yourself again.

And when it happens
whatever it is you're hiding

will come out
and believe me,

it will inspire you
to love yourself
again.

ROBERT M. DRAKE   80

FEELS FAMILIAR

And when I am
with you,

everything feels familiar.

Like two people
finding love

after a lifetime
of watching it

slip

through their hands.

WANT IT OR NOT

The soul prays,
whether you know it
or not.

There is a divine signal
coming from the middle
of your brain,
where all the atoms break.

Believe in this,
that the soul prays
and when it does
it asks for all the things
you're asking for

whether you're asking
or not.

Believe in this,
when good things happen,
when bad things happen.

When tears flood
through your eyes
and when laughter
swells your lungs.

Believe that the soul prays.
Believe that it prepares you

for all things

whether you want it
or not.

Believe in this.
Believe in words,
feelings,
and things you cannot see.

Like signals,
symbols,
and the way your heart
breathes.

It is true,
that the soul prays,
whether you know it
or not.
Believe in this
before you go.

Believe that all things
that happen . . .

come to us
whether we want it
or not.

ENOUGH IS NEVER ENOUGH

There is enough
human suffering in you
to collapse a building . . .

so why cause damage
to other people?

Why pain,
hate, and tears?

Why not love,
kindness, and laughter?

I know it's difficult
but the effort
is worth a place
in the sun.

Love hard
and love broken people
even harder.

OF COURSE

Yes, of course,
I could survive on my own.

I could swim,
run, think, and break
without the help
of other people.

I love myself
and I have always looked out
for myself
the best way I know how.

But I swear,
sometimes I feel the urge
to be held,
understood, and loved

in the sweetest way.

Sometimes,
I do need someone
to talk to,
to hold on to,
to love, and to live with
as well.

Sometimes,
I just need someone
to lean on over
and whisper:

*"I can't see
another day
without you*

*and I need you
in my life
just as much*

*as you need me
in yours."*

That's all.

BEST KIND . . .

Everyone is going to see you
how they see you
no matter what you do
or say.

No matter how good
you are
or how bad things get.

You are you,
so keep slaying, baby.

Self-love
is the best kind
of love

and there's no doubt
about that.

DISTANCE 2

Distance is more
than two objects apart.

It is the struggle
we all go through
when the heart
and the mind

can't seem
to get along.

I AM NOT SORRY

I'm sorry
I'm cold with you.

I'm sorry
at times,
I don't know what to do
or what to say.

And I'm sorry
I never have
the right words
for you.

It's just,
I've dealt with hearts
that don't break
too lightly.

Hard hearts, you know . . .
hearts that have seen
too much,

felt too much
to even flinch
a little
when it all goes wrong.

And I've dealt
with fragile hearts, too,

ones that shatter
the moment the air shifts
away from them.

Yes, life is hard
and loving someone
is even harder,

and right now
you caught me
at a difficult time
in my life,

a time
where I put myself first.

A time
where I only have
my own problems
to care about,
to deal with.

Yes, it is true,
I know it sounds selfish,

but I love who I am
and because of that,
I don't want to sugarcoat
how it is . . .

that is,

if the world is fucked up
then that's how
I want you to see it,
you know?

I won't protect you
from the truth,
from what hurts.

I'm not afraid
to make you feel bad
at the cost of being honest,

at the cost
of being myself.

Shit,
as if we don't have it
bad enough already.

And yes,
I know the both of us
have let go
many people,

both good and bad,
and because of it,

if I must break you,
then I will.

And if you must
break me . . .
then so be it.

I love you,
and I'm ready

no matter what you do
or what you say.

I am here.
I am here.
I am here.

And I
have nowhere else

to go.

IT FEELS THE WAY IT FEELS

It hurts . . .
of course it does,
because we were
made to hurt.

To feel.
To try to understand
even when we know
we cannot.

It hurts . . .
of course it does,
and at times,
we won't know
what to say,

but we will try
even if the words
are hard to project.

It hurts . . .
of course it does,
to watch you,
the people
we care about
go through hell

and not having
the power
to heal them
the way we should.

It hurts . . .
of course it does,
to breathe memories,

the ones
that take you back
to a place
when it all made sense.
Where the fire of pain
was smaller
than it is now.

It hurts . . .
of course it does,
as it always does.

When love isn't enough,
strong enough
to save the one you need.

It hurts . . .
of course it does.

The solitude.
The ache.

The longing
to be understood

and

the craving
of human interaction . . .

of touch,
of laughter,
and watching it
slip before
our naked eyes.

My dear,
it hurts,
all of it,
of course it does . . .

And the wounds
are deep enough,
they always are.

And they will always
hurt a little more
than before.

My dear,
it hurts,
believe that you
cannot outrun this.

Abandon this.
Destroy this
pool of feelings.

Understand,
how pain
is the curse
that will tear you apart
but also,
the blessing
that will bring us all
closer together.

Understand
that sometimes
life isn't beautiful.

That sometimes
life is hell

but we'd rather feel
the chaos

than feel

nothing
at all.

ABOUT YOU

You have so much
inside of you.

Like a thousand oceans
and a thousand moons

and here you are . . .

hurting over something
you'll soon grow out of . . .

something

you'll soon forget.

So why carry this pain?

When all the love
in the universe dwells
within you.

Find it.

The happiness you're seeking

begins
and will always

begin . . .

with you.

I OFTEN . . .

I often think
of whom it is
you are thinking of

right before

you go to sleep

and sometimes

I wonder
if it is me.

I wonder,
and I cannot say
this better myself

but I miss you,
and I hope you find
my precious company

when you feel
most alone.

THE THING ABOUT YOU

The thing about you is,
you carry this kindred sadness
that draws me in
and it's a lot like mine.

It peeks from the edge
of my eyes
when it wants to
and only a handful of people
take notice.

And it's the same way
I'm noticing yours
and *that's a beautiful thing.*

It's a miracle when similar people
find one another
and that's why
I've got to know you,

that's why
I've got to break you down,
to see if you love
the same way
as I do . . .

to see
if I'm really
not meant

to be alone.

MOMENT OF SILENCE

Let us thank
the lovers for being
lovers

and the haters
for giving us the courage,

the motivation,
and the fire

to keep on.

IN ALL MY . . .

In all my years
I have learned
that most people
never tend to change.

That most people
are meant to do
the same things,

feel the same things,
and even say
the same things

over and over.

And what is sad
about that is,

how those same people
don't get it.

They don't think
anything of it,
that is,
not growing
and not moving forward

only staying right
where they think
they belong.

They can't find peace,
and they find themselves
in the chaos
of the past.

Hell,
I don't want to die
the same as I did
when I was born.

I don't want anything of it.

If I taste love twice
then please
do not let it be the same.

If I feel heartbreak,
disappointment,
pain and even more,
then please
by all means,
do not let them arrive
in unison.

I want the chaos of life
in different times
and different stages
of my life.

I want to be old
and still feel the bitter sting
of letting go

and the sweet science behind
holding on.

I want to grow strong
and I want the wisdom
of a thousand men.

All I want is my life
to have meaning,
in all forms,
shapes, and sizes.

I want life.
I want life.
I want life.

I want it at all costs
even if it means . . .

I am doomed to
go through
the same things
more than twice.

BROKEN PEOPLE

I yearn for broken things.
For the things
that make drunk lovers

fall into each other
in the middle of the night

and the things
that keep them up

while the rest of the world
is asleep.

I love you,
I need you to break me,
and I don't want you
to apologize
for it

at all.

THINGS YOU FEEL

It hurts
because there are some things
you can't fake.

Like the feeling you get
while watching someone
you love
leave
without saying good-bye.

It hurts
because no matter
how many times you wake up,
you're still stuck in a world
where they glorify violence
rather than peace.

It hurts
because everyone around you
wants change
but no one has the courage
to change for themselves.

It hurts
because you have so much in you
but don't have the slightest clue
on how to pour it out.

It hurts
because you're up every night
thinking
why does it hurt
so damn much
without knowing why.

And lastly,
it hurts
because feelings matter
and you could never run
far enough

from all the things
you feel.

WHO YOU ARE

After all,
the world is made up
of different kinds of people,

so sooner or later
you're going to run into someone
just like you
and you're going to analyze them
and say,

*"Damn, I am complicated
but I am also beautiful."*

And that will be enough
to inspire you
and give you the perfect amount
of courage

to continue being
who you are.

CALL YOU

I'm sorry for the nights
I forgot to call you

and for the moments
we could have shared.

I'm sorry for letting you down
and for the several years
that have passed

without having the courage
to let you go.

I'm sorry for the way
I entered your life

and for the way I left
without granting you
a good-bye.

I'm sorry for all the mistakes
I've ever done

and for not doing enough
to make you stay.

I'm sorry,
and every night
I feel this way
and every night

I die to rise to go through
the same ordeal
as the night before.

Goddamn it,
now you have me here,
between four walls
wiping dry tears,

exhausting whatever light
I have left in me.

I need you
or I think I do
but none of that
is going to bring you back.

I just want you to know
that I'm sorry

for whatever pain
I might have left behind

and I hope one day,
you find it within you
to forgive me
for everything

I might have
caused.

THE LAST WORD

I want to change
the way you feel
about pain.

I want to show you
how not all hurting
is bad.

How sometimes
broken things
are beautiful things

and how sometimes
you need a little ache
to help you appreciate . . .

the gentle poetry
you create

with your beating heart.

A GIRL FROM THE PAST

She thinks of falling
outside
where the dead leaves pile.

She thinks falling
there
will save her.

She thinks each leaf
is a metaphor

for all the fallen lovers
who couldn't survive
her storm.

There she waits
for the rain.

There she waits
for the sadness
to go away.

There she waits
to be reborn,
to be loved,
and for someone
who might have enough
courage to stay . . .

no matter how much
of a danger
her heart is.

She's a moon
and she needs a man
with a heart

the size of an ocean
to pull her away
from the chaos
within.

The end.

the gift

the first shot.

She's tired of giving the wrong people the right pieces of herself. She looks at the one she loves and silently screams within her own mind. She feels stupid at times, but in all honesty, the only one stupid within this situation is the one too stupid to comprehend her love. Some men are not really men or, simply, they're not man enough to treat a woman the way she deserves. It's not your fault that you fell for someone who could say the right things yet fail to act on what they've expressed. You're not weak. Why? Well because you're strong enough to love even when that love isn't returned. Your love is unconditional and beautiful. Your love maintains its beauty even when you're stuck in an ugly, unhealthy relationship, and you still maintain your value even with someone who fails to value you.

Your smile is a symbol of your strength. Broken
is what you've felt but that isn't who you are.
I want you to know that your love is a flower
waiting to blossom, only to be shared with
someone devoted enough to only pick you from
a garden where only the truth can grow. Every
failed relationship was just an opportunity
for you to learn what to avoid as you begin to
preserve yourself for the one who deserves a
space in your life.

She is good enough, she is beautiful, she
is almighty and majestic. She is strong and
intelligent. She is a Queen deserving of more
than what she has had. She is you, and when you
discover the type of love that mirrors your own,
hold on to it.

the second shot.

i think you should leave him

i think you know this already

but you're afraid to start over

you're afraid of being alone

but don't you feel alone

whenever you're near that person

don't you feel like

there's something more

out there for you

i think you deserve more

but you already knew that

and i think you're strong enough

to walk away

from anyone undeserving of your energy

i believe that you are mighty enough

to separate yourself from the people

who are less than you deserve

because you are, in fact,

powerful enough to free yourself

from those who want to keep you in bondage

the third shot.

What if I told you that you were wasting your
time, sitting there waiting for a call that'll never
come from someone who never even deserved
to reach you? What if I told you that the love
you've been craving does not live in the heart
of the person you've been losing sleep over?
All those restless nights, and for what? You
could be asleep dreaming dreams that make you
smile; instead you sit there all alone in a dark
room gently lit by the moon, feelings of being
stuck in a nightmare that seems to be playing
on loop. It feels like the walls are closing in on
you, the ceiling is collapsing. Time is passing,
the night sinks into itself, and you become a
little less sure of everything you were already
questioning.

What if the love of your life is alone, just like
you, feeling some of the same feelings? With
questions as big as yours and doubts as deep
as the doubt that now consumes you? What if
holding on to someone who no longer deserves
your attention is distracting you from being with
the one person who would never hurt you in the
ways you've grown accustomed to? You could
really be in love instead of pretending to be in
love with someone who does nothing to earn
the love you've been wasting on the person who
isn't the one you should be with.

the sleeping city.

they say New York City never sleeps
but i've seen it close its eyes
like a child too tired to fight slumber

i've seen this city empty itself
like a soul craving nothingness
and a heart growing numb

it's almost 2 a.m. and the streets
feel like a ghost town
there are moments after midnight
where i often hear no sound

the sirens aren't screaming
on this particular night
just the hum from the wind
and a chill in the air

in just a few hours
the whispers will begin again
the cabs will stampede
down a one-way path
stopping for those who are prepared
to be transported
into the chaos of the city

but until then
the city that never sleeps
is barely awake
and i've stayed up to witness it

one hell of a midnight.

i hear the angels

their voices like the rain

touching, tapping my window

begging for my attention

as i lie here, weighed down by sadness

unable to move beneath the madness

the misery is so heavy

the misery is so thick

i hear the angels

but i can't see them

i hear the angels

but i can't move

this must be hell

this must bc the place

my mother warned me about

this must be the place

i swore i'd never visit

but i'm here

and for some reason

it feels like home

i hear the angels

but they won't reach me

on my second glass of whiskey.

You don't even know how much love you've
stolen from yourself while trying to maintain
unhealthy relationships with people who have
proven time and time again that they'll never
be able to love you the way you deserve. You
don't even know how much time you've robbed
yourself of. All those late nights and early
mornings, spent chasing the thought of a person
who rarely even thought about you.

You don't know, and I wish you did. I wish the
love you wasted on others would somehow have
found its way back to you, but you've insisted
on finding someone new after every person
you lose, not realizing they were never actually
losses because you never had them in the first
place. I wish you knew that they were never
losses because they were never valuable enough
to be that, but you were always everything, and
you were always giving your everything to a
person who insisted on doing nothing, giving
nothing. Using you up until they deemed you
to be empty every time they were finished. You
don't even know, but I wish you did, or maybe
you'll finally get it after reading these words.

you need to feel.

Your joy is constantly fading because you've
built your happiness on temporary things.
Your peace has now become reliant upon a
weak foundation. Sadly, you'd rather pretend
to be happy, smiling in photos, crying when
the lights of social media are off. Giving the
world a fictional version of who you are, hiding
your truth to appease others, your sadness is
not a burden. Your sadness is significant. Your
sadness is important. This thing that you feel
will strengthen your soul if you let it. So feel
whatever it is that you need to feel. No matter
what it is, you don't have to be silent.

you wear the sadness.

the joy is replaced with sadness

your expectation becomes disappointment

the truth was just an attractive lie

a bunch of letting, forming words

that came together to create sentences

of manipulation

the heart becomes cold

as if to lose its summer

the soul becomes tired

you and your restless spirit

what's behind those dead eyes

you wear that blank expression

like new skin

you wear sadness like the latest fashion

you wear pain like garments

you've been draped in anguish

don't you miss who you were

before who you became

took over your life

do you miss yourself

like i miss you

do you even remember

what it felt like to be happy

have you forgotten yourself

beneath your troubles

and all of this for a love

that turned out to be hatred

all of this for a heart

that never deserved yours

all of this hurt

for a relationship

that would never work

all of yourself

all of everything

invested into something

that now feels like nothing

22 minutes in a neon room.

i was searching for you
while you chased
after someone who wasn't me

i was in love
with the idea of knowing you
before i knew you

living in the hell
that i labeled love
while dying to meet
the one in my dreams

not realizing

at the time

that in order to begin

with you

i had to first end it

with any and everyone

incapable of loving me correctly

and you

would only find me

once you decided

to go after more

than you settled for

LAX.

the airport
filled with scattered emotions
some sadness, some pain
some joy, some relief

babies strapped on tight
to their mother's chest
the old man sitting in front of me
struggles to rest

so many stories playing out
the airport reads like a book
people searching for silence
reading words in a nook

the airport is alive
and it thrives on our souls
the airport is an exhibition
a production, a show

anxious.

uneasy in a room

filled with others

smothered by crowds

anxious from the noise

heard in raging halls

bouncing off the fucking walls

i wish to be alone

hidden behind silence

isolated by peace

away from everything

Feb 22nd.

there was a hole in the ceiling
and our room was too small
to house all of our things

the account was nearly overdrawn
and the stress from it all
felt like tons weighing upon
our fragile shoulders

we were broke
we were broken
we were tired
but we had each other
and that was the richest feeling

we didn't have much
but we had everything
when together

drunk beneath a pale moon.

I'm in a room, a dark room. Surrounded by
candles, the light is flickering off the wall. The
flame dances to the silence and the sound of
me breathing. I feel alone, nearing loneliness,
alone, overthinking. I feel sadness lurking near
the windows of my heart as the wrong thoughts
overcrowd my mind. I can't sleep, and so I just
lie here with my eyes searching the ceiling for
an imperfection, tracing old lines in the paint
that give off this illusion of the foundation
cracking. This is something I can relate to, being
imperfect, feeling as if I'll crack beneath the
weight of it all.

a nightly regret.

i regret being silent
i should've said more
but i kept quiet
blaming myself
being weighed down
by the shame of what happened

i trusted you
i shouldn't have
i allowed you in
i let you get close
to places
you never deserved to be
and you violated me

the betrayal has been heavy

so much that i struggled

to carry myself

suffering from the feeling

of coming undone

i regret being silent

but here i am

made stronger from the pain

more powerful than before

ready to tell the world

i refuse to be silent anymore

something to mentally consume.

I think you want to be the one who changes him.
You want to be the one who he gets it right with.
You've been heavily invested, and now he's
taken advantage of it. I don't think he respects
you in the way you deserve, and now that you've
allowed him back into your life countless times,
he doesn't take you seriously. I think he believes
that no matter what, you guys will just start up
again. It's time to teach him a lesson, and it's
time for you to preserve yourself for something
better.

Just think about this . . . life is too short. Are
you willing to give up a lifetime of real love
for someone who would rather give you a life
of pain and sadness? You have the power to let
go . . . find it . . . use it. Save yourself.

save me not.

I think I wanted you to save me. I waited for
you to breathe life into my fragile body and
aching soul. I was lying there, eyes closed, my
heart rate slowing down under the pressure of
trying to survive for us. I was lying there, lying
to myself while you continued to lie to me. You
never tried for me, but for some odd reason,
I always believed you would. Holding on to a
heavy hope, searching for a "yes" in a room
filled with everything that screamed "no." They
say love is blind, but I've come to understand
that was never love, and you were never the
love of my life. Instead, you would later become
the reason for the death of our union and our
existence together, and so I lie here, staring at
the ceiling. No longer willing to live for you or
us, I am ready to live for myself and the future
that will go on without you.

alone near you.

there were days where i considered you a soul mate

but it turns out the love of my life was just a lie

that i allowed myself to believe in

out of fear of being alone

not understanding that i felt the loneliest

whenever standing beside you

young and eager.

so often we give our firsts
to people who will forget us
as soon as something new arrives

so many special moments
wasted on people
who will never appreciate
the memories we gave them

i just wish someone
would have taught me
that waiting would be far more rewarding
than believing the liars
who only told me what i needed to hear
just to get what they always wanted

this almost endless journey.

you want so badly
to find the hands
worthy of touching you

you've traveled
to the very ends
of heartache
searching for a love
that would calm
the storms living
within your soul

you're just tired
of the raging fires
blazing through
the forest in your heart

eager to plant seeds
of love and watch them grow
because you deserve that much

awake, this nightmare.

we were reduced to pictures
in a broken frame
we became the memories
i'd force myself to forget
and you would become
my greatest regret

i miss the life i knew
before knowing you
i made the worst decision
in choosing you

a purple sky and glowing moon.

Travel beneath the surface of her exterior and
physical structure, and discover what is covered
by a guard in place to protect against anyone
who doesn't deserve to peek into the windows
of her soul. Earn the opportunity to meet her
there in her innermost vulnerability, and have a
conversation with her soul if you're man enough
to do so.

I want to speak to her soul, while others are
overly eager to touch her physically. I'd like to
stimulate the wires of her mind and live there
for a lifetime. I dream of dreams that only
consist of a woman like her, a woman like you.
Let me enter, but only when I am worthy of the
key that leads to you, leading me.

the beginning of another end.

where do promises go

when broken

what happens to love

when hearts are shattered

what happens to the truth

that was once given to a liar

we lose these things for one another

then search for them later

to give to someone else

and so it all begins again

the journey of friends

becoming lovers

then enemies in the end

315360000.

i've spent so much of my life
searching for the truth in liars
begging for love at the knees
of a person who hated being with me
waiting for a call that wouldn't come
holding on to the same hand
responsible for my bruises

i've spent so much of my life
unable to live, unable to breathe
needing someone who didn't want me
chasing after the ones who always walk away
claiming to be in love
when really, i was living in a version of hell
that i accepted because deep down
i didn't really think that i deserved
to have all the things i claimed to want

i've spent so much of my life

afraid of being truly happy

while wishing for happiness

lying to myself

pretending to be happy with lovers

who refused to love me

a city being heard.

i love the way the streets of New York
can make chaos look beautiful
the way the winters paint the city cold
forcing me to wrap my arms
around my lover, pulling her close

i fall in love with the Empire State Building
while drinking coffee, standing near the window
looking down to the ground
searching for that maddening sound
of sirens and car horns
the sounds of humans rushing
trying to survive, the hustlers hustling
trying to reach the things that seem out of reach

i love the way the city speaks
it yells out loud, refusing to be quiet
letting its power be heard
i hear it, i crave it, i listen

2/1.

this year

say "no" more often

stop trying for those

who never try for you

choose yourself

whenever others

refuse to choose you

stop settling for a love

that hurts your heart

focus on your goals

your career

never compromise your ambition

for an unhealthy relationship

2/19.

don't distract her from being great

don't interrupt her peace of mind

if you're not man enough

to stand firm beside her

don't waste her time

don't even speak to her

2/20.

It hurts right now, you're tired of going through
the same old shit. Your heart is weary, but you're
still powerful. Strong enough to walk away,
strong enough to make it without the person you
thought you needed.

2/21.

You know what's sad and ultimately fucked up?
You say you want real love, but your significant
other is fraudulent. You say you want to be
happy, but you insist on holding on to a person
who ruins your life. I wish you'd love yourself
more.

truly transformative.

she turned sadness into art

she turned pain into pure strength

she took what little they gave her

and made it more valuable

always and over again.

and that's the problem, love

you're constantly trying

to save the same man

who could never keep

your heart safe

connection means more.

anyone could give me attention

but i needed more

what i craved the most

was a never-ending connection

with the person

i had always been searching for

wasted years 2005.

Years of feeling like I could never be enough,
and yet I continue to try for you. My best efforts
made to look like nothing, forcing myself to stay
put. Content with a love life that feels like death.
There's no rest for the broken. I know that all
too well as I swell up from the abuse, the torture
of fighting for someone who would rather
fight against me than stand by my side when
it's time to go to war. What am I waiting for?
With nothing but sores to show. These wounds
and bruises, these scars are caused by you. My
fucked-up logic, wanting love but incapable of
finding it inside a relationship that feels more
like a situational mess.

I tried my best. I try and I try and die some
more then again I ask myself, "What have I been
fighting for?" Screaming out "Choose me or
you'll lose me" but I've yet to leave. Wanting us
to work but at the same time realizing that you
will never be able to provide all that I need. I see
and yet I'm blind all at the same time. My mind
overflows like great floods consuming cities.
Sometimes I wonder, if I leave you: Would it
hurt? Would you miss me? All this history and
yet nothing to truly show. Years of feeling like
I could never be enough for you has caused so
much damage to my fucking soul.

only a climax, nothing more.

It always begins with a lie. Some lonely soul told
a bunch of bullshit that sounds pretty enough
to believe. You never truly see it coming until
they're done coming. The climax marks the end
of something you were made to think would
last forever, but it was only for the moment, and
you were only a tool in assisting them to find
pleasure. It always begins with a lie, some false
comfort. True intentions wrapped up in a box
with so many bows that you deem it believable,
and you never see the truth until it's over and
you're left there alone, back where you began.
Trying to figure out how to piece yourself back
together.

tend to your devices.

cell phones make people invisible

haven't you noticed?

no you haven't

your attention redirected to a screen

making everything else obsolete

phone in hand, attention robbed

and those who sit among you

feel neglected

and one day you'll regret this

until then

your only friend

seems to be

the device you've chosen to hold

that thing you'd rather look at

instead of me

but see, maybe it's not your fault

child of a golden age of distractions

forced into a space

where you'd rather face a screen

than look at me

relating through sex.

how sad, lonely, and haunting
it must be
to only be able
to relate to others through sex

pretending to be okay
with being used
by those who don't deserve
to lie beside you

how sad it must be
to pretend that not caring
is some skill to be proud of
all because you've chosen
to settle for less than
what you deserve
pretending that it's everything
you've ever wanted

and so, you find yourself

in the arms of lovers

incapable of actually loving you

how sad and lonely

you must feel

pretending to be fine

while wasting your energy and time

wasted years 2014.

eventually my heart
stopped beating for you
it took some time
but my heart stopped aching for you

they say moving on is difficult
but so many say this without truly trying
without actually making an effort
to walk away from everything
that no longer deserves their presence

and so i took my things
left behind what i couldn't carry
i burned most of what we had
and the rest got buried

scary at first
but staying where i wasn't appreciated
would've been worse

i needed more of what
you refused to provide
i wanted to be with someone
who was nothing like you

from 15.

they play like loops
from my apartment window
i observe from 15 floors
above the ground

the people running late
people running toward their train
conversations floating in the cold air
sirens sounding off
like melodic screams for attention
my city is alive
my city is wide awake
even when the sun
chooses not to show its face

i see it every day
people running in circles
like a vinyl playing
my favorite song

43 degrees.

i may not know you

but i know your pain

i know that feeling that lives

beneath your bones

i know the madness that lives

within your brain

consuming your mind

like a virus craving chaos

and destruction

holding the ability to take away

your power to cultivate your own joy

peace no longer lives with you

or sits beside you

there is a type of emptiness

that dwells in the pit of your stomach

it makes you sick

it forces you to feel weak

you lose sleep because of this

you've lost yourself because of this

i may not know you by name

but i know exactly how you feel

i am familiar with the aches and the cracks

that remain on display

on the surface of your heart

i know the hell of searching for angels

where only devils dwell

i know exactly how it feels to seek warmth

during a cold, dark, emotional winter

i know enough about pain to know

that things get better

or maybe they actually don't

maybe, just maybe you get stronger

you'll get stronger

ludicrum 1.

if he's no good for you

then choosing to live a life

by his side

will mean choosing

to live in an endless version of hell

ludicrum 2.

you were never meant

to be someone's secret

you were always meant

to be loved out loud

ludicrum 3.

you only mattered when i cared
but i learned to stop giving life
to relationships that deserved to die
and i decided to stop giving life to you

ludicrum 4.

you were just an example

of everything

i learned to avoid

ludicrum 5.

i'm not searching for a love

that makes me blind

i want a love

that helps me see

i want a love

that opens me up

to everything i've always

wished for

ludicrum 6.

aren't you tired of always being the one
they cheat with
aren't you tired of being on the side
of the person who only sees you
as someone to just keep on the side

aren't you tired
of being the one
they call when they're done
fucking somebody else

ludicrum 7.

my father was the first man

to betray me

he was also the first person

to break my spirit

took time.

I believe I wanted more of everything that you were incapable of giving me. I thought I lost you, but today I realize that I only gained the chance to be truly happy after you left. I found the type of peace that had always escaped me in our relationship, and now that we are over, I am sober enough to walk this straight line of living a life that no longer includes you.

ludicrum 8.

i used to live for us

and now you're dead to me

ludicrum 9.

we're not sleeping just to rest

we're closing our eyes

just to escape the things

that haunt us while we're awake

ludicrum 10.

how she fought through the fire

was all that mattered

watching a woman survive

is something you never forget

like you, this moment.

There will be nights where you'll struggle to
sleep, you'll reach for your phone, and your
pain will bring you here, to this moment, these
words. There will be nights where your soul will
long for more and your mind will crave a peace
that feels like freedom. There will be nights
where you'll grow weary of being kept awake by
the thought of someone who no longer deserves
to be on your mind, and in this moment, as you
read these words, I hope you find the strength
to remove yourself from a relationship with
someone who doesn't deserve to be the reason
you can't sleep, and I hope you realize that you
are not alone because there are so many souls
reading this while struggling to find rest.

Just like you . . .

ludicrum 11.

there are moments

where she feels as if

she's falling apart

she is unraveling

and yet she is still strong

she is still powerful

a silent awakening.

there's a type of freedom
that lives in a space of solitude
the mind is free to roam
without seeking permission
and in that moment
you find yourself more available
and readily able to choose yourself
without feeling guilty or selfish

where there is solitude
there is a deeper understanding
and appreciation for peace and joy

sometimes you have to be alone
in order to discover what truly matters

ludicrum 12.

you'll be fine
you'll make it
not because of a man
or a relationship

you'll get through this
because you have yourself
and right now
you are everything you need
and you have always been enough

this, still vivid.

i remember you
or maybe i've been recalling
the person i thought you were

your beautiful lie
the empty compliments
my willingness to believe
in something or someone
who was pretending to feel
the same way as i did

the pain is still vivid
i bury the anguish with a smile
i drown out the sound of crying
with music that reminds me of you

i remember the way it felt

my heart beginning to swell

my soul near drowning

my mind inching further into madness

that part is still vivid

that part of me that ended

in a dark, empty room

under a midnight moon

breaking into a million pieces

over a person who was never

what they promised to be

ludicrum 13.

It won't be easy, it'll be difficult, but this will
be the year she finds herself. This will be the
year she discovers the power and magic living
beneath her bones. This will be the year where
she begins to walk away from anything that no
longer deserves her presence.

rare, not many.

Women like you are hard to come by. Women like you are gems, rare diamonds hidden on the top of the highest mountains. There's only a few of you in existence; there's not many of you left. You have a fire in your soul that will never be put out and a heart consumed with a power strong enough to calm hurricanes. You deserve so much more than the mediocre bullshit that you've decided to settle for. You're always providing, trying, and fighting. It's time for someone to fight for you.

sinking ships.

i think the silence replaced our screams

we sat there preserving our energy

for other things, maybe even other people

we stopped touching each other

eye contact was obsolete

as we continued to drift apart

like a ship leaving the shore

i wanted more

and you deserved something different

our friends tried to warn us

but we never listened

i think it went too far this time

no more screaming

no more yelling

i think the silence replaced everything

we knew before

we were no longer willing

to fight for each other

lack of lessons.

who taught you to settle

for a love that wasn't love

who failed you

which parent failed you

who in your family

decided to betray you

by failing to teach you

about the troubles in this world

and the evil in men

now here you are

an adult struggling

to find yourself

lost beneath the crumbling foundation

that should have been made stronger

by the people who raised you

they failed you . . .

ludicrum 14.

she, a flower

blooming under

her own light

and even when alone

she had everything

she needed

ludicrum 15.

the roses make death

look beautiful

the way they die

with grace

gone by daylight.

like the stars embedded

into the night sky

she belonged to the moon

and she was never yours

to keep

ludicrum 16.

kind, dead eyes

pale, dry lips

forcing themselves

to smile

tired but wide awake

broken yet strong

struggling to find peace

in a moment of emotional chaos

ludicrum 17.

the screams are usually silent
hidden behind closed doors
heavily guarded
for fear of being judged

all those dreadful emotions
kept secret on pages of journals
afraid to speak about it
so you write it down
and this is how poetry is born

too early, the heartache.

What do you say to a girl who becomes familiar
with heartache before she's legal enough to
drink? What are words to a girl who is used
to getting hurt by everyone claiming to care?
All these young souls drowning in sadness
before knowing how to swim. Trying to
navigate this rugged terrain called life. Sadly,
heartbreak arrives earlier than it should, but if
there's anything that I know for sure it is that
the heartache transforms the broken girl into
a powerful woman. I just wish the pain didn't
start so young. I just wish you had more time
to comprehend what it means to be happy and
maybe one day you will.

ludicrum 18.

let yourself move on
to a better chapter
it's time to turn the page
to a story worth reading

the painful pursuit.

Chasing love, I'm tired. Wired and awake,
restless and weary. My heart can't take another
tumble to the floor. My mind still aches from
all this overthinking. It's overwhelming the way
this pursuit of everything I deserve only brings
me more of what I don't want. I've been chasing
you, and I'm tired.

one day too late.

Did you not see the way she looked into your eyes, as if your pupils held the answers to all of her questions? Did you not feel the way she held your hand tight, as if she was holding a bag filled with every promise ever made?

This love was rare, heartfelt, and true. She was ready and willing to lay down her life for you, but it's too bad you couldn't see it. Blinded by flashes of attention by everyone who wasn't her. You'll understand when it's too late. You'll understand when you go searching for her replacement and you find out that she was the only one of her kind.

oh well.

You hate me for being able to articulate
something that you struggle to find the words
for. You are angry with me for having the
ability to express the truths that others keep
hidden with a smile. This is not your story, you
don't own the copyright to the pain I speak of,
the heartache is universal, and I don't know if
you're aware of this, but you're not the only one
hurting. Maybe you're mad at me, or maybe
you're mad at the women who choose to read my
words instead of yours.

needed me.

i needed truth

i needed substance

i needed passion

i needed love

i thought i needed you

but turns out

i only needed me

because i was everything

you couldn't appreciate

i was everything

you didn't deserve

and i'll be everything

for myself

ludicrum 19.

i saw the moon during the day

and it reminded me

that nothing is impossible

because sometimes

nothing can stop the moon

from witnessing the sun

effort meant nothing.

i was always hurting myself
to make sure you were good
compromising my peace
just to entertain the chaos
of loving you

my heart bound
by a one-sided love
unsure of what to do
paralyzed by lies
struggling to move

lies told to my reflection.

you tell yourself enough lies
and you'll stay a bit longer
pretending to be happy
smiling on cue, posing for photos
wearing joy like a mask
while struggling to find peace

you put on your best face today
and even though it's getting worse
you'll say "i'm fine" if anyone asks

you tell yourself enough lies

and you'll hold on a bit longer

your hands begin to cramp

and hope becomes your worst enemy

as your grip becomes tighter

and it's clear that you don't love yourself

because loving someone who can't love you

is simply a harsh reminder

but you've told yourself enough lies

to keep you in a relationship

with someone who will never

be honest with you

the sad sister.

Your sick, sad sister slithers like snakes, saying
sorry without meaning it. Filled with envy,
she's painted the color green. Pretending to
love you the way a sister should but becoming
overwhelmed with rage when you're doing good.
She wants to control you, but she can't. She
wants to be you, but she can't. I think she swells
up with hatred because she can't fathom a world
where you become more than she is, and yet she
has to live in a world where you are greater than
she expected you to be.

forever never comes.

i've been standing here
waiting for more
of what you refuse to give
more of what you promised
more of what you've continued
to deny me

i've been standing here
waiting for the arrival
of the person i thought you were
i've been standing here
in the cold
waiting for you to warm me up
emotionally starving myself
with this impossible hope
that you'll eventually change

i've rearranged my entire life for you

for nothing it seems

my dreams are no longer dreams

the thought of you

has become a dreadful nightmare

as i stand here, staring into the abyss

awaiting something that'll never happen

i stand here alone and empty

waiting to be filled

by someone who has proven

to be full of shit

and though i should quit

i've chosen not to walk away

failing to realize

that not giving up on you

means giving up on myself

i stand here waiting

afraid, fearful of the unknown

scared to move

because what if you show up

and what if you arrive

as everything i wanted you to be

it's been days, now weeks, now years

and i'm still standing, i'm still here

ever-evolving.

Life evolves a bit faster when you've surrounded
yourself with high-frequency people, individuals
who push you to do more than you knew you
were capable of. People who have chosen to do
more, to be more and so they encourage those
around them to do the same. Understanding
this, I've chosen to remove the people from my
life who have done nothing but fill me up with
doubt, people who have knocked me down for
wanting more than I was accustomed to having.
I learned to keep my dreams out of the hands of
those who preferred me living in a nightmare.
I decided to walk away from everyone who
appeared to be threatened by my smile. You are
capable of changing your own life, but first you
have to let go of the people who'd rather see you
down than up.

you, a mountain.

do not let a world
filled with criticism
and judgment
prevent you from being
whatever you need to be

don't let the words
from those who don't matter
corrupt your peace of mind
do not allow them the power
to force you into corners
or uncomfortable spaces

reserve and maintain the right

to be happy despite

all that's happened

take back your power

and feel whatever it is

you need to feel in order to survive

do not be threatened by hills

when you yourself are a mountain

do not fear the rain

when you yourself are a beautiful storm

of chances and hope

with so much confusion.

Confused men are not worthy of your time.
Their confusion is an insult to your existence.
Why not have a partner who is sure about the
way you make them feel and isn't afraid to
express it rather than be with a person who has
grown content with pretending that they don't
want you? Claiming to miss you but never
showing up. Claiming to love you but choosing
to hurt your heart. Confused men are the muddy
puddles of the earth; don't let them stain your
soul.

how much longer.

you're just tired
you've been brave
you've never given up
you keep fighting
but you're tired

weary from all the arguments
weary from all the forgiveness
weary from all the second chances
you've been providing

you're strong
but you're just tired
of the type of love
that seems to keep you down
the type of feeling
that isn't love at all

this heaviness that sits

on your shoulders

it makes you stronger

but you're just tired

of trying to build a home

on quicksand

you're tired

but you're powerful enough

to let go

you may be tired

but you're still strong enough

to walk away

you may be restless

but you don't deserve

this nightmare

you're just tired

you've been brave

but it's time to choose yourself

because they're no longer

choosing you

i know, i know.

The modern era of love feels like hatred and happiness have become a mask we wear to hide the sadness that thrives in our heart. Honesty has become a lost art, and loyalty seems to have vanished right before our eyes. I've seen people fall victim to empty promises and apologies from liars. I've watched hearts become crushed under the weight of hoping for things that'll never come. I know what it means to reach for unclean hands and expect something pure. I know how it feels to feel all the right things for the wrong people. Too many games being played, too many moments gone to waste. Energy and trust misplaced, invested into those who will never be worth it or match your own value. I know what it means to be hurt in this era, and this is why I'll never judge a guarded heart.

so many drinks.

how many drinks
until i forget
all the things
that haunt me
while i'm sober

this temporary high
a moment of overcoming
my lows

only to be brought back down
to a reality in which i hate

i've tried lying to myself
i've barhopped, i've stood
in lines to get into clubs
in hopes of running away
from all this shit

but it comes for me
first thing in the morning
and sticks to me
like gum under a classroom desk
a fucking mess i've been

trying to win, giving in to sin
i've gained so many vices
pretending to love it
but i don't like this

so many drinks
but nothing changes
i don't want to be here
i need to change this

she, alone.

she nursed her own wounds
and as crazy as this may sound
every time she'd fallen to the ground
she picked up the pieces
and carried herself on her shoulders

she was nothing like they imagined
she was more than they claimed
she'd be

she fought on her own
she meant everything to herself
she took care of her own needs

the unstoppable force.

she was no princess

her distress didn't need

your attention

she was a warrior

fighting for herself

and everything she deserved

she refused to allow others

the ability to control her narrative

she produced and published her own story

and there was nothing

anyone could do to stop her

072288.

I don't judge people for wanting to disappear.
So many of us are hiding, looking for an exit,
eager to leave this all behind. I've been there
too, and there are times where I struggle with
this feeling, but I've fallen in love with life every
time I fall for you.

so full.

i saw a glimpse
of everything
i wanted to be
when i looked
into her eyes

this is when i knew
she was the moon
to my darkened sky

skhxxii.

your lips made me forget

my reason to be unhappy

you kissed me

and i lost that dreadful feeling

3/6.

stop apologizing to people

who have no problem

with hurting your soul

all this confusion

the madness of saying sorry

for feeling things

that you deserve to feel

things that you have a right

to express

apologizing to keep them happy

apologizing to keep people

who no longer deserve

to dwell within the walls

of your heart

you shouldn't have to suppress

your emotional truths

for people who don't

give a fuck about you

trust the moon.

the moon sat outside her window

like a lover waiting to be told

the secrets that remained

chained up in her heart

golden, her existence.

She was always amazing, she was nothing like
you'd ever known. The way she smiled through
the chaos, the way she held her own. Her soul
was always divine, her heart concealed magic.
Her entire existence was a constellation of
stars burning the dark hue of the night sky.
She was always this, but you could never see
it. She had always been a poem that you failed
to appreciate, and when you lost her, you lost
a future filled with promise and progression.
The lesson here is never chase copper when the
woman who loves you is golden.

the ice is cracking.

Life is too short to spend days on end dancing
around the inconvenient truth. The romance
you long for will never exist with this particular
person. You're chasing after a dream, avoiding
a sickening reality. Your eyes have been closed
while you wander upon thin ice, and it's time
that you wake up. It's time to stop giving all of
yourself to someone who gives nothing to you.

last call.

maybe she's tired of the clubs

maybe she's tired of searching for light

in the nightlife

dancing around in the dark

when she'd rather be at home

with someone who feels like home

maybe she's tired of the drinks

tired of getting lost in a bottle

tired of losing herself

in her pursuit of peace

running away from all the things

that haunt her

she is powerful

she is strong

she keeps fighting

she's still standing

but damn, she's still tired

ready for something new

something better

because this shit

isn't working anymore

maybe she's tired of the clubs . . .

more what-ifs.

What if I told you that I was here the whole
damn time? Waiting to be seen, eager to hold
and love you but you were too busy chasing
someone who wasn't me. Searching for love in
a relationship with someone who would rather
make you hate yourself. I was here the whole
time, but you were distracted, wasting your
energy on someone too weak to appreciate
you. The person you chose didn't deserve you.
The person you wanted was keeping you from
noticing me, and ultimately you missed a real
shot at happiness. All these fucking what-ifs . . .

All these missed opportunities to be loved

Because you'd rather put trust in a liar . . .

i wrote this for you.

Your heart is aching, but you pose and smile in
Instagram photos, pretending to have the time
of your life. Deep down you're hurting, trying
things and nothing's working, but you've grown
accustomed to acting like everything is perfect.
You're worth it, maybe you just forgot. Maybe
you're in like or in love with someone who treats
you like you're not. Maybe your heart has fallen
into hands too weak to hold it. Maybe you are
too proud, too bold, too embarrassed to show it.
Your soul aches beneath the weight of all this
emotional pain. Your soul continues to crack as
you continue to act as if everything is okay, but
nothing is okay and most of what is wrong is
now buried beneath the lies you tell yourself and
others.

I just wish you could see yourself in the light,
but you're used to this, being left in the dark.
Standing in the middle of chaos, trying your
hardest to keep it together. Clinging to that
relationship that should end, still hoping for a
forever. You deserve so much more, and deep
down you know this. Open your eyes, stand up,
please focus. Understand each and every word.
You are the reason I wrote this.

exit here.

All I wanted was for you to try. I was always
asking for too much whenever I was asking
you. Being made to feel needy by someone
who didn't need me. Believe me, I've gone back
and forth with myself over all of this. Plotting
ways to walk away in hopes of saving my own
heart. Ripped apart by my own inability to
see a life without you. Blind while with you,
damp tissues next to the bed, I play back all the
fucked-up things you said. Hurting my head
while overthinking, sinking into a pit of all the
shit I should forget. My greatest regret is that
I didn't leave sooner, couldn't leave sooner. I
let you trample upon my dreams, tearing me at
the seams. Your love was never what it seemed
or what you made it out to be. I believed lies
wrapped in paper labeled "truth." My life filled
with drama the moment I gave my heart to you.
Emotional abuse and plenty of excuses, hanging
on your every word like several criminals in
nooses. And now my soul is screaming, can you
hear it? Will you listen? I can't take this shit
anymore, I found the door, fuck it, I'm finished.

the gift index.

r.h. Sin   236

EMPTY BOTTLES FULL *of* STORIES

copyright © 2019 by Robert M. Drake and
r.h. Sin. Illustration copyright © 2019 by
Hannah Olson. All rights reserved. Printed in
the United States of America. No part of this
book may be used or reproduced in any manner
whatsoever without written permission except in
the case of reprints in the context of reviews.

Andrews McMeel Publishing
a division of Andrews McMeel Universal
1130 Walnut Street, Kansas City, Missouri 64106

www.andrewsmcmeel.com

20 21 22 23 24 BVG 11 10 9 8 7

ISBN: 978-1-4494-9647-0

Library of Congress Control Number: 2018950602

Editor: Patty Rice
Designer/Art Director: Diane Marsh
Production Editor: Amy Strassner
Production Manager: Cliff Koehler

Cover illustration by Hannah Olson

ATTENTION: SCHOOLS AND BUSINESSES
Andrews McMeel books are available at quantity
discounts with bulk purchase for educational,
business, or sales promotional use. For information,
please e-mail the Andrews McMeel Publishing Special
Sales Department: specialsales@amuniversal.com.